SIMPLY DE

Ice-creams
& Desserts

KÖNEMANN

Making the most of commercial ice-cream

With good quality commercial ice-cream and a few extra ingredients you can make delicious desserts in no time.

Espresso Coffee

Place 1 litre softened vanilla ice-cream in mixing bowl. Combine ¼ cup espresso instant coffee powder and 1 tablespoon water. Add to bowl and stir until smooth. Return to ice-cream container. Freeze overnight. Serve with chocolate discs.

Chocolate Hokey-pokey

Place 1 litre softened chocolate ice-cream in mixing bowl. Add 2 x 60 g chopped chocolate coated honeycomb bars. Mix until evenly distributed. Pour mixture into freezer container. Freeze overnight.

Ginger Honey

Place 1 litre vanilla ice-cream in mixing bowl. Combine 2–3 tablespoons chopped ginger in syrup, 1 tablespoon ginger syrup and 2 tablespoons honey in small pan. Stir over low heat until combined. Cool. Fold mixture into ice-cream. Pour into a container. Freeze overnight. Decorate with extra chopped glacé ginger.

Scorched Peanut

Combine 1 litre vanilla or chocolate ice-cream and 2 x 40 g roughly

chopped scorched peanut bars. Mix well. Pour into container. Freeze overnight. Top with extra chopped scorched peanut bars and biscuits.

Chocolate Rum 'n' Raisin

Place 1 litre chocolate ice-cream in mixing bowl. Combine $1/2$ cup chopped raisins and $1/4$ cup rum in small pan. Stir over low heat until all liquid is absorbed. Cool. Fold raisin mixture into ice-cream. Pour into a freezer container. Freeze overnight.

Left to right: Espresso Coffee, Chocolate Hokey-pokey, Ginger Honey, Scorched Peanut, Chocolate Rum 'n' Raisin, Fruit Swirl, Jaffa Chip.

Fruit Swirl

Place 1 litre softened vanilla or mango ice-cream in mixing bowl. Add 1–2 teaspoons grated orange rind; stir until smooth. Pour mixture into freezer container. Pour in $1/3$ cup mango or passionfruit pulp. Swirl with a skewer or knife to create a decorative marbled effect. Freeze overnight. When required, serve in scoops drizzled with passionfruit pulp.

Jaffa Chip

Place 1 litre vanilla ice-cream in mixing bowl. Add 2 teaspoons grated orange rind, 2–3 teaspoons orange juice, 2 teaspoons Grand Marnier and $1/3$ cup finely chopped dark chocolate. Mix well. OR combine vanilla ice-cream with $1/3$ cup chopped jaffas. Pour mixture into container. Freeze overnight. When required, serve in scoops with wafers.

3

Ice-creams

Simple to make, ice-creams are a delicious finish to any meal. Old-fashioned vanilla ice-cream will complement most desserts. Fruit, nut or chocolate ice-creams are delicious by themselves. For a special treat, try Lavender, Mango, Tropical or Brown Bread Ice-cream.

Old-fashioned Vanilla Ice-cream

Preparation time:
  30 minutes +
  freezing/churning
Total cooking time:
  10 minutes
Makes 1.2 litres

3/4 cup caster sugar
2 vanilla beans, split
  lengthwise
1 cup milk
6 egg yolks, lightly
  beaten
2 cups cream
caramel sauce and
  wafers for serving

1. Place sugar and vanilla beans in medium heatproof bowl. Pour milk over. Stand bowl over pan of simmering water. Stir milk mixture until simmering.
2. Remove milk from heat. Place yolks in heatproof bowl. Gradually add milk to the egg yolks and whisk through thoroughly.
3. Return mixture to heat over simmering water. Stir constantly over low heat until mixture coats the back of the spoon. Remove from heat, set aside to cool. Place plastic wrap over the surface of the custard to prevent a skin from forming. Stir cream through cooled custard and chill in refrigerator for at least 2 hours.
4. Remove vanilla beans from custard and scrape the seeds from the beans into the mixture, discard pods. Pour the custard into an ice-cream machine and churn for about 30 minutes or until ice-cream is firm.

Old-fashioned Vanilla Ice-cream (top)
and Ultra-rich Chocolate Ice-cream.

5. To make by hand: Prepare up to 4. Pour mixture into metal freezer tray and freeze 2–3 hours or until just solid around the edges. Remove. Transfer mixture to medium bowl. Beat with electric beaters until smooth. Return to freezer tray and freeze 3–4 hours or until firm. Serve with caramel sauce and wafers if liked.

Ultra-rich Chocolate Ice-cream

Preparation time:
  20 minutes +
  churning and freezing
Total cooking time:
  10 minutes
Makes 3 cups

1½ cups cream
½ cup milk
¼ cup sugar
100 g dark chocolate,
  chopped
3 egg yolks, lightly
  beaten
½ teaspoon vanilla
  essence
chocolate cups and
  white chocolate for
  serving

1. Place cream, milk, sugar and chocolate into the top of a double boiler or a heatproof bowl over pan of simmering water. Stir over medium heat until chocolate has melted and sugar has dissolved. Remove from heat. Cool slightly. Whisk in egg yolks and essence.
2. Pour mixture into ice-cream maker and allow to chill/churn for about 30 minutes.
3. When firm, serve, or store in an airtight container in freezer. Serve in chocolate cups with shavings of white chocolate.
4. **To make by hand:** Prepare up to 2. Pour into freezer trays, freeze until just solid around the edges. Transfer to a bowl, beat well. Pour into freezer container, leave until firm.

Lemon Ice-cream

Preparation time:
  20 minutes + freezing
Total cooking time:
  15 minutes
Serves 4–6

6 egg yolks
⅔ cup caster sugar
2 teaspoons grated
  lemon rind
⅓ cup lemon juice
4 egg whites
⅓ cup caster sugar, extra
½ cup cream, lightly
  whipped
lemon rind strips
  and strawberries
  for serving

1. Whisk or beat yolks in heatproof bowl. Stand over pan of simmering water; whisk until light and fluffy and increased in volume. Add sugar, rind and juice, continue whisking until thick and pale. Remove from heat, cool slightly.
2. Using electric beaters, beat egg whites until stiff peaks form. Add extra sugar gradually. Beat until sugar is dissolved and mixture is thick and glossy.
3. Using a metal spoon, fold egg whites and cream into lemon mixture. Pour into a 7-cup capacity metal freezer tray. Freeze 3–4 hours or until firm. Garnish with rind and strawberries.

Tropical Ice-cream

Preparation time:
  15 minutes + freezing
Total cooking time:
  Nil
Serves 4–6

1 litre commercial
  vanilla ice-cream
⅓ cup fresh or canned
  passionfruit pulp
⅓ cup orange juice
  concentrate
⅔ cup finely chopped
  mango or pawpaw
passionfruit pulp,
  extra, and fruit

Tropical Ice-cream (top) and Lemon Ice-cream.

1. Allow ice-cream to soften slightly.
2. Add passionfruit pulp and juice. Mash together with a fork.
3. Using a metal spoon, fold in mango or pawpaw. Return to the freezer for at least 6 hours or until firm. Serve scoops with extra pulp and fresh fruit.

Mango Ice-cream

Preparation time:
  25 minutes + freezing
Total cooking time:
  10 minutes
Makes 1 litre

4 egg yolks
2/3 cup icing sugar
2 cups mango purée
1 tablespoon lemon
  juice
1/2 cup coconut cream
1/2 cup cream
brandy baskets, fresh
  mango and shredded
  coconut for serving

1. Place egg yolks and icing sugar in a medium heatproof bowl. Stand over pan of simmering water, beating until eggs are thick and creamy. Remove from heat, continue beating for 1 minute longer or until cool.

2. Place mango purée, juice, coconut cream and cream into a large bowl, mix well. Using a metal spoon, gently fold in the egg mixture.

3. Spoon into an 18 x 27 cm or one-litre capacity rectangular tin. Store, covered with foil, in freezer 3 hours or until the mixture is almost frozen.

4. Transfer to large mixing bowl. Using electric beaters, beat on high speed until smooth. Return mixture to tin or container, store, covered with foil, in freezer for 5 hours or overnight. Scoop into brandy baskets, top with slices of fresh mango and shredded coconut.

Note: You can buy brandy baskets from gourmet delicatessens and major department stores.

Mango Ice-cream.

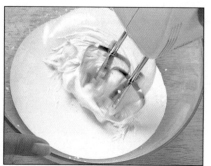

1. *Remove bowl from heat. Continue beating mixture 1 minute longer.*

2. *Using a metal spoon, gently fold in the egg mixture.*

3. Spoon into an 18 x 27 cm or one-litre capacity rectangular tin.

4. Using electric beaters, beat on high speed until smooth.

9

Kulfi

Preparation time:
10 minutes +
churning and freezing
Total cooking time:
10 minutes
Makes 1 litre

2 cups milk
¾ cup sugar
1 tablespoon cornflour
375 ml can evaporated
  milk
2 tablespoons chopped
  pistachio nuts
2 tablespoons chopped
  almonds
2 teaspoons rosewater
almond bread for
  serving

1. Place milk and sugar
into a medium pan. Stir
over low heat until
milk is almost boiling
and sugar dissolved.
2. Blend cornflour
with a little of the
evaporated milk and
stir into the milk and
sugar mixture. Stir over
low heat 3–4 minutes
or until mixture
thickens. Remove from
heat and allow to cool
slightly. Stir in the
remaining evaporated
milk, chopped
pistachios, almonds
and rosewater.
3. Pour mixture into
an ice-cream maker
and chill/churn for
about 30 minutes or
until firm.

4. *To make by hand:*
Pour prepared mixture
into freezer trays and
freeze until edges are
firm. Transfer to a bowl,
beat until light and
creamy, return mixture
to ice-cream tray, freeze
until firm. Serve with
almond bread.

Note: Orange or other
scented water, available
from supermarkets or
health food stores, can
be used instead of
rosewater.

Strawberry and Raspberry Ripple

Preparation time:
20 minutes + freezing
Total cooking time:
Nil
Serves 8–10

2 x 250 g punnets
  strawberries
1½ cups caster sugar
2 tablespoons lemon
  juice
2¼ cups cream, lightly
  whipped
125 g (½ punnet)
  raspberries
½ cup caster sugar,
  extra
raspberries and
  strawberries, extra,
  for serving

1. Line the base and
sides of a 7-cup
capacity loaf tin with
foil. Remove stalks
from strawberries.
Place in a food
processor with sugar
and juice. Process for
30 seconds or until
quite smooth.
2. Reserve one-third
cup whipped cream,
fold remaining cream
into strawberry
mixture. Pour into
metal freezer tray.
Freeze, stirring
occasionally until thick.
Do not allow mixture
to freeze solid.
3. Using a food
processor, blend
raspberries and extra
sugar. Fold into the
reserved cream and
mix well.
4. Spoon a layer of
strawberry ice-cream
over base of the
prepared tin. Spoon
raspberry mixture and
remaining strawberry
ice-cream randomly
over base. Using a
sharp knife or skewer,
swirl mixtures
together, being careful
not to dig into the foil.
Freeze for 3–4 hours
or overnight. May be
served in scoops or
removed from tin and
cut in slices. Garnish
with extra raspberries
and quartered
strawberries.

Strawberry and Raspberry Ripple (top) and Kulfi.

Coffee, Rum and Walnut Ice-cream

Preparation time:
  15 minutes +
  freezing and churning
Total cooking time:
  5 minutes
Makes about 1.5 litres

3/4 cup water
3/4 cup caster sugar
3 teaspoons instant
  coffee powder
2 cups cream
2 cups milk
1/4 cup rum
1 1/4 cups (150 g)
  toasted walnuts,
  roughly chopped
walnuts, extra,
  and wafers
  for serving

1. Place water, sugar and coffee powder in pan. Stir over low heat without boiling until sugar and coffee are both dissolved. Remove from heat, cool.
2. Combine cooled mixture, cream, milk and rum, mix well. Pour into an ice-cream machine, chill/churn for about 30 minutes.
3. When ice-cream is starting to thicken, add walnuts and chill/churn for a further 10 minutes. Serve with walnuts and wafers.

Praline Ice-cream

Preparation time:
  1 hour +
  overnight freezing
Total cooking time:
  25 minutes
Serves 6–8
(recipe may be doubled successfully)

4 eggs yolks
3/4 teaspoon vanilla
  essence
1 tablespoon sugar
1 1/4 cups (300 ml)
  reduced cream

Almond Toffee
1/4 cup sugar
1 tablespoon water
80 g slivered almonds,
  lightly toasted
1/4 cup cream,
  lightly whipped

Topping
3/4 cup cream, extra
1 teaspoon caster sugar
  (optional)
3 teaspoons brandy or
  Grand Marnier
strawberries for serving

1. Beat egg yolks, essence and sugar in medium mixing bowl until thick and pale. Heat reduced cream in pan until almost boiling; remove from heat. Add reduced cream gradually to egg mixture, beating constantly. Stand bowl in hot water for 10 minutes, stirring occasionally or until slightly thickened. Place bowl over pan of simmering water; whisk for 5 minutes or until thickened. Remove from heat. Cover surface with plastic wrap.
2. *To make almond toffee:* Line a tray with foil, grease lightly. Combine sugar, water and almonds in small pan. Stir over medium heat 3–4 minutes or until sugar dissolves. Cook without stirring for 5–10 minutes or until deep golden in colour. Do not allow to burn. Pour onto tray. Set aside until cold.
3. Finely crush the prepared almond toffee. Fold two-thirds of toffee into warm custard. Cool. When cold, fold through whipped cream.
4. Line a 21 x 14 x 7 cm loaf tin with a strip of foil. Pour in custard mixture. Freeze for 6 hours or overnight. Invert ice-cream onto serving platter.
5. *To make topping:* Beat extra cream and sugar until soft peaks form, fold in liquor. Spread over ice-cream. Sprinkle with reserved toffee, cut into slices. Garnish with strawberry halves.

---

*Praline Ice-cream (top) and
Coffee, Rum and Walnut Ice-cream.*

Rum & Raisin Ice-cream

Preparation time:
  5 minutes +
  overnight standing +
  churning and freezing
Total cooking time:
  Nil
Makes 1.5 litres

3/4 cup raisins, chopped
1/4 cup dark rum
2 cups cream
2 cups milk
3/4 cup caster sugar
1/2 teaspoon vanilla
  essence
strawberries for serving

1. Combine raisins and rum in a small bowl. Cover, stand overnight.
2. Place all ingredients except strawberries in a large bowl and mix thoroughly.
3. Pour into an ice-cream maker and chill/churn for 30 minutes.
4. *To make by hand:* Follow instructions up to step 3. Pour mixture into freezer trays and freeze until mixture is beginning to set around edges. Transfer mixture to a large bowl. Beat with electric beaters until mixture is light and creamy. Return mixture to freezer trays. Freeze for 3–4 hours or until firm. Serve with strawberry halves if desired.

Chocolate Chip Ice-cream

Preparation time:
  20 minutes + freezing
Total cooking time:
  12 minutes
Serves 6

3 eggs
2 tablespoons caster
  sugar
200 g milk chocolate,
  melted
1 1/3 cups cream
90 g dark chocolate,
  finely chopped
raspberries, chocolate
  sticks for serving

1. Place eggs and sugar in bowl. Stand over pan of simmering water, Beat or whisk until it is fluffy, pale and increased in volume.
2. Add milk chocolate, mix well. Remove from heat. Cool.
3. Using electric beaters, beat cream until soft peaks form. Fold into egg mixture. Add dark chocolate, mix well. Pour into metal tray (4-cup capacity), freeze 4–5 hours or until firm. Serve with raspberries and chocolate sticks.

Double Honey Ice-cream

Preparation time:
  15 minutes +
  4–5 hours
  freezing
Total cooking time:
  Nil
Serves 6–8

3 eggs, separated
1/3 cup honey
1 1/4 cups cream
2 x 50 g bars chocolate-
  coated honeycomb

1. Using electric beaters, beat egg yolks in a bowl until light and fluffy. Add honey, beat until mixture is thick and pale.
2. Beat cream until stiff peaks form. In a clean, dry bowl, beat egg whites until stiff peaks form. Using a metal spoon, fold cream into egg whites. Fold into honey mixture.
3. Chop one of the honeycomb bars into small pieces and stir through the ice-cream. Pour mixture into 5–6-cup capacity container. Freeze for 4–5 hours or until firm. Serve scoops garnished with second honeycomb bar chopped in pieces.

Clockwise from left: Rum & Raisin Ice-cream, Double Honey Ice-cream and Chocolate Chip Ice-cream.

Peach Ice-cream

Preparation time:
12 minutes +
3–4 hours freezing
Total cooking time:
9 minutes
Serves 8

1¼ cups cream
4 egg yolks
¾ cup sugar
500 g peaches
1 tablespoon lemon
juice
2 tablespoons sugar,
extra

1. Heat cream in a pan until almost boiling. Remove from heat.
2. Beat or whisk egg yolks and sugar in a medium bowl until thick and pale. Gradually add the hot cream, beating constantly. Return mixture to pan. Stir over low heat 5 minutes or until mixture thickens. Do not boil. Pour into a bowl, leave to cool, stirring occasionally.
3. Reserve one peach, peel remainder and chop into pieces. Place in a food processor with lemon juice and extra sugar. Process 20 seconds or until finely puréed. Stir into

the custard. Pour into a metal tray (5-cup capacity). Freeze for 3–4 hours or until firm or churn in an ice-cream machine according to the manufacturer's instructions. Serve scoops garnished with slices of fresh peach.

Christmas Ice-cream Pudding

Preparation time:
about 1 hour (spread over a couple of days)
Total cooking time:
Nil
Serves 10

⅓ cup (50 g) toasted
almonds, chopped
¼ cup mixed peel
⅓ cup (60 g) raisins,
chopped
⅓ cup (60 g) sultanas
⅓ cup (60 g) currants
⅓ cup rum
1 litre commercial
vanilla ice-cream
2 tablespoons brandy
½ cup (100 g) red and
green glacé cherries,
quartered
1 teaspoon mixed spice
1 teaspoon ground
cinnamon
½ teaspoon ground
nutmeg
1 litre commercial
chocolate ice-cream

1. Place almonds, peel, raisins, sultanas, currants and rum in a medium bowl. Mix well. Cover with plastic wrap. Stand overnight. Place a 2–litre capacity pudding basin into the freezer to chill.
2. Soften the vanilla ice-cream slightly and mix in the brandy and cherries. Press this ice-cream around the inside of the chilled pudding bowl, spreading evenly right to the top of the bowl. Return to freezer and freeze overnight. It might be necessary to check the ice-cream a couple of times and respread evenly to the top if required.
3. Next day, add spices and chocolate ice-cream to fruit mixture; mix well. Spoon into the centre of the pudding bowl and smooth the top.
4. Return to freezer overnight or until very firm. Serve cut into wedges decorated with holly leaves.

> **HINT**
> Christmas Ice-cream Pudding is a refreshing substitute for the traditional hot pudding. It can be varied using your favourite fruit and nuts.

Peach Ice-cream (top)
and Christmas Ice-cream Pudding.

Brown Bread Ice-cream

Preparation time:
  25 minutes +
  freezing time
Total cooking time:
  10–15 minutes
Serves 6

2 egg yolks
⅓ cup caster sugar
½ cup longlife milk
1½ cups finely grated
  fresh brown
  breadcrumbs
1¼ cups cream
1 tablespoon rum
orange rind for garnish

1. Whisk egg yolks and sugar in bowl until pale and creamy. Heat milk in pan until simmering, but not boiling. Carefully pour milk over the yolk mixture, whisking constantly.
2. Return mixture to pan and cook custard gently over low heat, stirring constantly until mixture lightly coats the back of a wooden spoon, remove from heat. (Do not boil or it will curdle.)
3. Transfer mixture to a bowl, fold in the breadcrumbs. Cover with plastic wrap, cool.
4. Beat cream until soft peaks form. Stir in rum. Carefully fold cream into cold custard. Pour into attractive serving or freezing container, freeze until lightly frozen. Serve in dessert dishes or parfait glasses, garnished with strips of orange rind. There is no need to use a commercial ice-cream machine for this recipe.

Note: Dried commercial breadcrumbs are not a satisfactory substitute for fresh breadcrumbs.

Brown Bread Ice-cream.

1. Using whisk, beat egg yolks and sugar in bowl until pale and creamy.

2. Stir custard constantly until it lightly coats the back of a wooden spoon.

3. *Transfer mixture to a bowl and fold in finely grated breadcrumbs.*

4. *Beat cream until soft peaks form, stir in rum. Carefully fold into cold custard.*

Passionfruit and Pistachio Nut Ice-cream

Preparation time:
15 minutes +
  overnight freezing
Total cooking time:
15 minutes
Serves 8

½ cup milk
1½ cups cream
6 egg yolks
1¼ cups caster sugar
pulp of 8 passionfruit
⅓ cup shelled pistachio
  nuts, chopped
canned passionfruit
  pulp for serving

1. Heat milk and cream in a medium pan until almost boiling.
2. Using electric beaters, beat yolks and sugar in medium bowl until pale and thick. Add the milk and cream gradually, stirring until well combined. Return mixture to pan. Stir constantly over medium heat until lightly thickened; do not boil. Transfer mixture to a bowl. Cool, stirring occasionally.
3. Reserve one quarter cup of passionfruit pulp. Place remainder in small pan. Warm over medium heat for 1–2 minutes. Remove from heat; strain. Add passionfruit juice and reserved passionfruit to cream mixture. Pour into metal tray (6-cup capacity), freeze 3–4 hours or until just frozen around edges.
4. Transfer mixture to large bowl. Beat with electric beaters until thick and creamy. Add pistachios, mix well. Return to freezer. Freeze overnight or until firm. Serve with passionfruit pulp.

White Chocolate Ice-cream

Preparation time:
  20 minutes + freezing
Total cooking time:
  20 minutes
Serves 10

200 g white chocolate
¾ cup sugar
½ cup water
½ teaspoon cream
  of tartar
4 egg whites
2 cups cream
¼ cup brandy
chocolate wafers,
  strawberries and dark
  chocolate for serving

1. Grate or coarsely chop the white chocolate.
2. Place sugar, water and cream of tartar in a medium pan. Stir over a low heat without boiling until sugar has dissolved. Bring to boil, reduce heat slightly, boil without stirring for 15 minutes or until a teaspoon of mixture dropped into cold water reaches soft-ball stage. Allow mixture to cool slightly.
3. Using electric beaters, beat egg whites until soft peaks form. Gradually pour in syrup in a thin stream over egg whites; beating constantly until mixture is thick and glossy.
4. In a medium bowl, beat cream until soft peaks form. Fold whipped cream into egg white mixture. Add the white chocolate and brandy, mix well.
5. Pour into a metal tray (9-cup capacity). Freeze for 4–5 hours or until firm. Serve with chocolate wafers and strawberry halves. Sprinkle with grated dark chocolate.

Passionfruit and Pistachio Nut Ice-cream (top)
and White Chocolate Ice-cream.

Lavender Ice-cream

Preparation time:
25 minutes + freezing
Total cooking time:
Nil
Serves 6–8

2 tablespoons fresh
  lavender flowers
  stripped from their
  stalks
2 tablespoons sweet
  white wine (such as
  sauterne, muscat,
  Beaumes de Venise)
2 cups (500 ml)
  reduced cream
*1/2 cup (110 g) lavender
  or vanilla caster sugar
  (see* Note*)
2 egg whites
2 tablespoons fresh
  lavender flowers,
  extra*

1. Combine lavender
flowers and wine in a
small bowl; leave in a
warm place for about
5 minutes to allow the
flavour to develop.
2. Using electric beaters,
beat cream until stiff
and glossy. Gradually
mix in strained wine
with half the sugar.
3. Beat the egg whites
until stiff peaks form,
beat in remaining sugar.
4. Using a metal spoon,
fold egg whites into the
cream with extra
lavender flowers. Spoon
mixture into a bowl or
tray, freeze 3–4 hours or
until just firm. Serve
scoops in tuile baskets.

Note: Dried lavender is
often suggested in
recipes such as this, but
there can be a bitterness
from the volatile oils.
Fresh lavender does not
have this bitterness. To
make lavender or
vanilla sugar, place
fresh lavender or a
vanilla bean into a jar
of sugar. The flavour
will be absorbed by
the sugar.

Ginger and Roasted Almond Ice-cream

Preparation time:
3 minutes + freezing
Total cooking time:
15 minutes
Serves 6–8

*1/3 cup (60 g) whole
  blanched almonds
1 1/2 cups cream
1/2 cup milk
6 egg yolks
2/3 cup caster sugar
1/4 cup very finely
  chopped glacé ginger
sweet pretzels and glacé
  ginger for serving*

1. Preheat oven to
moderate 180°C. Place
almonds into a small
shallow cake tin and
roast for 8 minutes or
until golden brown.
Remove from oven.
When almonds are
cool, chop them
roughly.
2. Heat cream and
milk in medium pan
until almost boiling.
Remove from heat.
Beat or whisk egg
yolks and sugar in
large bowl until thick
and pale. Gradually
add milk, beating
constantly. Return
mixture to pan. Stir
over low heat for
5 minutes or until
mixture thickens.
Do not boil. Remove
from heat.
3. Stir in ginger, allow
to cool.
4. Pour into a
metal tray (6-cup
capacity)and freeze
or churn in an ice-
cream machine
according to the
manufacturer's
instructions. When
partly frozen, add
nuts and mix through.
Return to freezer until
firm. Serve topped
with sweet pretzels
and sprinkled with
glacé ginger.

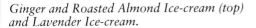

*Ginger and Roasted Almond Ice-cream (top)
and Lavender Ice-cream.*

23

Sorbets

Here is a selection of wonderfully simple sorbets and gelatos. Sorbets made from fresh fruit or juice with champagne, wine or liqueur can be served between courses to refresh the palate or as a light dessert. Gelatos are slightly richer and are always served as a dessert. Try Vanilla, Rich Chocolate or Orange.

Blackberry and Raspberry Sorbet

Preparation time:
  40 minutes +
  freezing time
Total cooking time:
  15–20 minutes
Serves 8–10

6 *cups blackberries or*
  blackcurrants
  (fresh or frozen)
2 *cups raspberries,*
  (fresh or frozen)
2 *cups water*
1 1/2 *cups sugar*
1–2 *tablespoons*
  lemon juice
2 *egg whites*
lime rind for serving

1. Place blackberries or blackcurrants, raspberries and half the water into large pan. Bring to boil, reduce heat. Simmer gently for 2 minutes or until pulpy. Strain through fine muslin sieve. Return strained mixture to pan. Add remaining water.
2. Add the sugar and lemon juice and stir over low heat until the sugar dissolves. Remove from heat. Allow to cool.
3. Pour mixture into freezer trays and freeze until sorbet is a mushy consistency. Using electric beaters, beat egg whites until stiff peaks form. Using a metal spoon, fold egg whites into berry mixture. Freeze, stirring occasionally to ensure egg whites are evenly distributed.
4. May be served in scoops or scraped for serving. Garnish with finely shredded strips of fresh lime rind.

Vanilla Gelato (top)
and Blackberry and Raspberry Sorbet.

Vanilla Gelato

Preparation time:
  10 minutes +
  churning and freezing
Total cooking time:
  Nil
Makes 1 litre

4 cups milk
1 cup caster sugar
1 1/2 teaspoons vanilla
  essence
sweet almond bread
  for serving

1. Place all ingredients except almond bread into an ice-cream machine and chill/churn for 30 minutes or until firm.
2. *To make by hand:* Combine all the ingredients in a bowl, mix well. Pour mixture into metal freezer trays and freeze until just firm around the edges.
3. Remove from freezer and beat with electric beaters or process in food processor until the mixture is creamy and smooth.
4. Return to freezer trays and freeze for 3–4 hours or until firm. Serve with almond bread if liked.

Note: Do not allow the gelato to become too hard before removing for beating.

Rich Chocolate Gelato

Preparation time:
  15 minutes +
  churning and freezing
Total cooking time:
  5 minutes
Makes 1.5 litres

4 cups milk
1 1/4 cups sugar
1/2 teaspoon vanilla
  essence
1/4 teaspoon instant
  coffee powder
150 g dark chocolate,
  chopped

1. Place milk, sugar and vanilla into a large pan, stir over low heat without boiling until the sugar has dissolved.
2. Remove from heat and stir in the coffee and chocolate. Continue to stir until chocolate has melted and mixture is smooth.
3. Pour into an ice-cream maker, chill/churn for about 30 minutes or until gelato is firm.
4. *To make by hand:* Follow instructions up to 3. Pour mixture into a metal freezer tray and freeze until mixture is set about 2.5 cm around edges. Transfer mixture to a large bowl. Beat with electric beaters until thick. Return to freezer trays and freeze 3–4 hours or until firm.

Strawberry Sorbet

Preparation time:
  15 minutes + freezing
Total cooking time:
  5–10 minutes
Makes 3 cups

1 cup sugar
1 cup water
1 cup fresh strawberry
  purée

1. Place sugar and water in a medium pan. Stir over a low heat until sugar has dissolved. Remove from heat and allow to cool.
2. Combine strawberry purée with the cooled sugar syrup and pour into a metal freezer tray. Place in freezer.
3. Freeze for 3–4 hours or until mixture is beginning to set around the edges, remove from freezer. Transfer mixture to small mixing bowl. Using electric beaters, beat until smooth.
4. Return mixture to tray and refreeze until gently set. Serve with extra strawberries and whipped cream if liked.

Strawberry Sorbet (top) and Rich Chocolate Gelato.

Jasmine Sorbet

Preparation time:
 15 minutes +
 freezing
Total cooking time:
 Nil
Makes 1 litre

2 cups strong jasmine
 tea
³/4 cup pure icing sugar
1 tablespoon chopped
 fresh mint
1 tablespoon lemon
 juice
2 tablespoons orange
 juice
1 egg white
strips of orange rind
 for garnish

1. Strain the hot tea
over combined icing
sugar and mint in a jug.
Stir until the sugar has
dissolved. Stir in the
lemon and orange juice
and allow to cool.

2. Strain the mixture
into a metal freezer tray
and freeze for about 2
hours. Remove from
freezer. Transfer mixture
to small mixing bowl.
3. Using electric beaters,
beat until smooth.
Return mixture to tray
and freeze for 1 hour.
Place mixture in a
medium mixing bowl.
4. Using electric beaters,
beat egg white until soft
peaks form. Fold gently
into the sorbet. Return
to freezer until firm.
Serve in scoops or
scrape into serving dish.
Garnish with rind.

Hint
Other flavoured teas
such as chamomile
or peppermint may
be used to make
sorbets. Combine
them with your
favourite herbs
and flavourings.

Jasmine Sorbet.

*1. Stir in the lemon and orange juice and
allow to cool.*

*2. Strain the mixture into a metal freezer
tray and freeze for about 2 hours.*

3. Using electric beaters, beat the mixture until smooth.

4. Fold beaten egg white gently into the sorbet. Return to freezer until firm.

Champagne Sorbet

Preparation time:
15 minutes +
freezing or churning
Total cooking time:
5–10 minutes
Serves 4–6

2/3 cup sugar
1/2 cup water
1/2 cup orange juice
1 1/4 cups brut
  champagne or
  a good quality
  sparkling wine
1 egg white, lightly
  beaten
grapes for garnish

1. Combine sugar and water in a medium pan, stir over low heat without boiling until sugar dissolves. Remove from heat. Refrigerate until cool. Add orange juice and champagne or wine. Whisk in egg white.
2. Pour into freezer trays and freeze 2 hours or until mushy. Transfer mixture to mixing bowl. Beat with electric beaters until smooth. Return to freezer 5–6 hours or until firm.
3. Scrape sorbet into champagne flutes or goblets to serve.
4. *To make with an ice-cream churn:* Pour mixture into machine after champagne is added and churn until beginning to freeze. Add the beaten egg white and continue to churn until sorbet is ready. Because of the sugar and alcohol levels, this sorbet is slow to freeze, so allow plenty of time.

Note: May be served between courses or as a delicate dessert. A pretty way to garnish is to frost a tiny bunch of seedless grapes with a lightly beaten egg white and caster sugar. Place these on the goblet with a very small grape leaf.

Orange Gelato

Preparation time:
30 minutes +
churning and freezing
Total cooking time:
20 minutes
Makes 1 1/2 litres

1 1/4 cups pure icing
  sugar
1 1/2 cups freshly
  squeezed orange juice
2 cups water
1 tablespoon lemon
  juice
2 tablespoons
  Cointreau or Grand
  Marnier
2 egg whites
1/4 cup icing sugar, extra

1. Place icing sugar, orange juice, water and lemon juice in a large pan. Stir over medium heat 4–5 minutes or until sugar is dissolved. Bring to boil. Reduce heat. Simmer gently for 15 minutes; remove from heat.
2. Pour into a large bowl, allow to cool. Stir in liqueur.
3. Using electric beaters, beat egg whites until soft peaks form. Gradually beat in the extra icing sugar until thick and glossy.
4. Using a metal spoon, gently fold egg whites into orange mixture. Pour mixture into an ice-cream machine and churn for about 30 minutes or freeze until just solid.
5. *To make by hand:* Prepare up to step 3. Before adding egg whites, pour the mixture into a freezer tray and freeze until beginning to set around the edges.
6. Remove from freezer and beat well. Beat egg whites to soft peaks. Add extra sugar. Beat well. Fold into orange mixture. Return to tray and freeze until firm. Serve with slices of orange.

Orange Gelato (top) and Champagne Sorbet.

Simple Citrus Sorbet

Preparation time:
30 minutes +
freezing
Total cooking time:
5–10 minutes
Serves 6–8

1 tablespoon gelatine
1¹/2 cups cold water
¹/2 cup boiling water
1 cup sugar
1 cup lemon, orange,
   grapefruit or lime
   juice (or a
   combination of
   all three)

1. Sprinkle gelatine over ¹/2 cup of the cold water in medium pan. Stand for 10 minutes. Add the boiling water and stir over low heat until gelatine is dissolved.
2. Add sugar and stir without boiling until sugar is dissolved. Remove from heat.
3. Add remaining cold water and the strained juices. Refrigerate. Pour into freezer trays and freeze 2–3 hours or until just firm.
4. Scrape or scoop frozen mixture into chilled dessert dishes or wine glasses. May be garnished with small citrus leaves or shreds of lemon, lime and/or orange rind.

Passionfruit and Orange Sorbet

Preparation time:
15 minutes +
churning and freezing
Total cooking time:
Nil
Makes about 1 litre

3 cups orange juice
³/4 cup passionfruit pulp
¹/2 cup caster sugar
2 tablespoons Grand
   Marnier
2 egg whites

1. Combine orange juice, passionfruit pulp, sugar and Grand Marnier in a large bowl. Using electric beaters, beat egg whites until soft peaks form.
2. Using a metal spoon gradually fold egg whites into orange juice mixture; pour into ice-cream machine and chill/churn for about 30 minutes.
3. Serve in scoops in a chilled bowl, garnish with candied oranges and a sprig of mint.
4. *To make by hand:* Prepare the mixture as above and pour into freezer trays. Freeze until just firm around edges. Do not allow to become too firm. Scrape into a bowl and

beat until light and fluffy. Return to trays and freeze for 3 hours or until firm.

Kiwi Fruit Sorbet

Preparation time:
30 minutes + freezing
Total cooking time:
5–10 minutes
Serves 4–6

6 large kiwi fruit
¹/3 cup sugar
1 cup water
2 egg whites

1. Peel and chop kiwi fruit. Combine in pan with sugar and water. Stir over low heat without boiling until sugar has dissolved. Bring to boil. Reduce heat, simmer 5–10 minutes until fruit is soft. Remove from heat. Cool slightly.
2. In food processor, process kiwi fruit in batches until smooth.
3. Using electric beaters, beat egg whites until firm peaks form. Fold egg whites into kiwi fruit mixture. Pour into freezer tray, freeze 3–4 hours until almost frozen. Transfer to bowl. Using electric beaters, beat until smooth. Freeze overnight.

Clockwise from left: Simple Citrus Sorbet, Kiwi Fruit Sorbet and Passionfruit and Orange Sorbet.

Deswerts

A special feature of your meal can be chosen from these enticing recipes. For a rich, full flavour, try Charlotte Malakoff, for a lighter texture, Zabaglione. Or try good old favourites Baked Rice Custard or Crème Caramel.

Black Forest Gateau

Preparation time:
1 hour 20 minutes
Total cooking time:
45 minutes
Serves 6–8

125 g butter
1/2 cup caster sugar
1/2 cup icing sugar
2 eggs, lightly beaten
1 1/2 teaspoons vanilla
  essence
1 1/2 cups self-raising
  flour
1/2 cup cocoa powder
1 teaspoon bicarbonate
  of soda
1 cup buttermilk
1 tablespoon vegetable
  oil
1 1/2 cups cream,
  whipped
425 g can pitted
  cherries, drained
200 g butter,
  extra
200 g dark chocolate,
  melted

1. Preheat oven to moderate 180°C. Brush a deep, 20 cm round cake tin with melted butter or oil. Line base and sides with paper; grease paper. Using electric beaters, beat butter and sugars in small mixing bowl until light and creamy. Add eggs gradually, beating thoroughly after each addition. Add essence, beat until well combined. Transfer mixture to a large mixing bowl. Using a metal spoon, fold in dry ingredients alternately with buttermilk and oil. Stir until just combined and mixture is smooth.
2. Pour mixture into prepared tin; smooth surface. Bake for 45 minutes or until skewer comes out clean when inserted in centre. Leave cake in tin for 10 minutes before turning onto wire rack to cool.

Black Forest Gateau.

3. To assemble cake:
Using a serrated knife, cut cake horizontally into three layers. Place first layer on serving plate. Spread with one-third of the cream. Top with half the cherries. Continue layering ending with cream on top.
4. Beat extra butter with electric beaters until light and creamy. Add chocolate, beat until smooth. Spread evenly around the sides of cake. Pipe rosettes or swirls around the outer edge of the cake. Decorate with cherries and chocolate curls.

Crème Caramel

Preparation time:
25 minutes +
refrigeration
Total cooking time:
35 minutes
Serves 8

Caramel
1 cup sugar
1/4 cup water

Custard
4 cups milk, warmed
1/2 cup sugar
6 eggs
11/2 teaspoons vanilla essence

1. To make caramel:
Preheat oven to

moderate 180°C. Brush eight 1/2-cup capacity ovenproof ramekins with melted butter. Place sugar and water in medium pan. Stir over low heat until sugar dissolves. Bring to boil, reduce heat and simmer 5–10 minutes or until mixture turns caramel. Remove from heat. Pour a little hot mixture over base of prepared dishes and swirl to cover base.
2. To make custard:
Place the milk and sugar in a pan and stir gently over low heat until sugar has dissolved. Whisk together eggs and vanilla for 2 minutes, stir in warm milk. Strain mixture into jug.
3. Divide egg and milk mixture between the moulds and place in a baking dish. Pour in hot water to come halfway up the sides. Bake for 30 minutes until custard is set and a knife comes out clean when inserted Cool, refrigerate at least 6 hours before serving.
4. To unmould, run a knife around the edge of each custard and gently upturn onto the serving plate. Shake gently if necessary. Serve with whipped cream and strawberries if liked.

Melon in Passionfruit Ginger Syrup

Preparation time:
30 minutes
Total cooking time:
10–15 minutes
Serves 4–6

pulp of 2 passionfruit
1/4 cup sugar
1/2 cup water
2–3 teaspoons shredded ginger in syrup
1 teaspoon finely chopped fresh mint
1/2 large rockmelon
1/2 watermelon
1 honeydew melon or pawpaw

1. Combine passionfruit, sugar, water and ginger in medium pan. Stir over low heat without boiling until sugar has dissolved. Bring to boil, reduce heat, simmer 10–15 minutes or until slightly thickened. Remove from heat. Add mint, allow to cool completely.
2. Remove seeds from melons. Using a melon baller, scoop balls of flesh from fruit. Arrange fruit in serving glasses or dishes. Pour syrup over. May be served with freshly whipped cream or ice-cream.

Melon in Passionfruit Ginger Syrup (top) and Crème Caramel.

1. Dip sponge fingers into combined liqueur and water.

2. Using a metal spoon, fold in cream and almonds.

Charlotte Malakoff

Preparation time:
1 hour + chilling
Total cooking time:
Nil
Serves 8–12

250 g pkt Italian
  sponge fingers
¹/₂ cup Grand Marnier
  or other liqueur
¹/₂ cup water
2 x 250 g punnets
  strawberries, hulled
  and halved
whipped cream and
  strawberries for serving

Almond cream
125 g unsalted butter
¹/₃ cup caster sugar
¹/₄ cup Grand Marnier
  or other liqueur
¹/₄ teaspoon almond
  essence
³/₄ cup cream, whipped
³/₄ cup ground almonds

1. Brush a deep cake tin or mould (1–1.5 L capacity) with melted butter or oil. Line base with greaseproof paper; grease paper. Trim sponge fingers to fit sides of mould, reserving trimmings. Dip sponge fingers into combined liqueur and water. Arrange around the side of the mould in an upright position.
2. *To make almond cream:* Using electric beaters, beat butter and sugar until light and creamy. Add liqueur and essence. Continue beating until mixture is smooth and sugar is dissolved. Using a metal spoon, fold in the cream and almonds.
3. Spoon one-third of the almond cream into base of the mould. Cover almond cream with strawberry halves.

Top with a layer of sponge fingers. Continue layering, finishing with a layer of sponge fingers; press down.
4. Cover with foil, place a small plate and weight on top. Refrigerate for 8 hours or overnight. Remove plate and foil and turn onto chilled serving plate. Remove greaseproof paper. Decorate with whipped cream and strawberries.

> **H**INT
> One of the desserts in the "grand tradition", this is very rich and should be served after a light main course. It is splendid to serve when you invite guests for coffee and cake, rather than for a meal. It is lovely for a party.

Charlotte Malakoff.

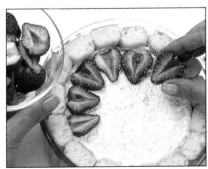

3. Arrange strawberry halves over the almond cream.

4. Cover with foil, place a small plate and weight on top.

Simmered Blueberry and Port Sundae

Preparation time:
15 minutes
Total cooking time:
5–8 minutes
Serves 4

2–2¹/2 cups fresh or
frozen blueberries
¹/4–¹/2 cup sugar
(depending on
tartness of berries)
¹/2 cup port (or muscat)
1 cinnamon stick,
broken in two
1 tablespoon brandy
scoops of rich vanilla
ice-cream

1. Place blueberries
into small pan with
the sugar, port and
cinnamon stick.
Simmer very gently
over low heat for
2–8 minutes or until
berries are tender.
2. Remove from heat
and add brandy. Serve
warm or cold.
3. Place scoops of ice-
cream into sundae
dishes. Top with
simmered blueberries.
Whipped cream may
be passed around
separately with this
dish if liked.

Note: For ease of
serving, freeze scoops
on a tray until solid.

Mud Cake

Preparation time:
40 minutes
Total cooking time:
2–2¹/4 hours
Serves 8–10

2 cups sugar
1¹/4 cups plain flour
1 cup self-raising flour
¹/2 cup cocoa powder
¹/2 teaspoon
bicarbonate of soda
4 eggs, lightly beaten
1 cup buttermilk
1 teaspoon vanilla
essence
pinch salt
300 g butter, melted
300 g dark chocolate,
finely chopped
white chocolate for
serving

Icing
200 g dark chocolate,
chopped
¹/3 cup cream

1. Preheat oven to slow
150°C. Brush a deep
23 cm round cake tin
with melted butter or
oil, line base and sides
with baking paper.
2. Place sugar in large
mixing bowl. Add
sifted flours, cocoa and
soda. Make a well in
the centre. Using a
metal spoon, fold in
combined eggs,
buttermilk, essence
and salt. Stir until well
combined.
3. Add butter and
chocolate, mix well.
Pour mixture into
prepared tin and
smooth surface. Bake
2–2¹/4 hours or until
skewer comes out clean
when inserted in centre
of cake. Leave cake in
tin until cold, turn onto
wire rack (this cake
cracks on the top).
Using a serrated-edged
knife, cut dome off top
of cake horizontally.
Turn cake upside
down. Stand cake on
wire rack over paper-
lined tray. Pour icing
completely over cake
and smooth top and
sides, using a flat-
bladed knife. Allow
to set. Transfer cake
carefully to serving
plate. Serve in wedges
with whipped cream,
garnished with strips
of white chocolate.
4. *To make icing:*
Combine chocolate and
cream in a small pan.
Stir over low heat until
chocolate has melted
and the mixture is
smooth. Remove from
heat. Cool.

Note: Mud cake is
delicious served warm
or cold and is a treat
for afternoon tea.

---

*Simmered Blueberry and Port Sundae (top)
and Mud Cake.*

Dobos Torte

Preparation time:
55–60 minutes
Total cooking time:
40 minutes
Serves 12

8 eggs, separated
1 cup caster sugar
1¹/2 cups plain flour

Filling
1¹/2 cups caster sugar
¹/2 cup water
5 egg yolks
¹/4 cup cocoa powder
100 g dark chocolate,
  melted
250 g unsalted butter

Toffee
1 cup caster sugar
¹/2 cup water
125 g flaked almonds,
  toasted

1. Preheat oven to moderate 180°C. Line six baking trays with baking paper and draw a 23 cm circle on each sheet of paper. Using electric beaters, beat egg yolks and half the sugar for 20 minutes or until thick and pale. Beat egg whites until stiff peaks form. Gradually add remaining sugar, beating until thick and glossy and sugar is dissolved.

2. Sift flour onto the beaten egg yolks. Using a metal spoon, fold in gently. Fold in egg whites one-third at a time until completely folded through the mixture.

3. Spread the mixture evenly onto the circles on prepared trays and bake for 6–9 minutes or until lightly golden and the top of each cake springs back when lightly touched. Turn onto wire racks and allow to cool. When cooled, trim edges of cakes evenly.

4. *To make filling:* Place sugar and water in a medium pan. Stir until sugar is dissolved. Bring to boil, reduce heat and simmer 10–15 minutes or until the syrup reaches soft-ball stage. Using electric beaters, beat egg yolks in a medium bowl. Gradually pour the hot syrup onto the egg yolks in a thin stream, beating constantly, and continue beating until mixture is cool and thick. Add cocoa, beating until smooth. Add melted chocolate to the mixture, beating until well combined. Beat the butter until

light and creamy, gradually add egg mixture to the butter mixture until blended and smooth.

5. *To make toffee:* Place sugar and water in a heavy-based pan, stir over low heat until sugar is dissolved. Boil without stirring 5–10 minutes or until the syrup changes to a golden colour. Pour onto one of the cakes. Spread the caramel quickly and evenly and, while still soft, cut into 12 equal wedges with a hot, oiled sharp knife.

6. *To assemble:* Spread the filling over remaining cakes, reserving sufficient filling to cover the sides. Sandwich the cakes one on top of the other and place the caramel layer on top. Spread the sides evenly with the filling mixture and press toasted almonds around sides of the cake. Cut into wedges to serve.

HINT
This dessert is best left to stand for a day or two before serving. Flavours will be absorbed into the cake.

Dobos Torte.

Crème Brûlée

Preparation time:
15 minutes +
3 hours refrigeration
Total cooking time:
1 hour
Serves 4

1 vanilla bean, split in
   half lengthways
2 cups cream
4 egg yolks
1/3 cup sugar
2 tablespoons soft
   brown sugar

1. Preheat oven to
moderately slow
160°C. Place vanilla
bean and cream in a
medium pan. Stir over
low heat until cream
begins to simmer.
Remove vanilla bean,
scrape seeds into the
cream and set aside.
2. Lightly whisk the
egg yolks and sugar
together until thick and
pale. Gradually add the
cream, whisking gently.
3. Strain the mixture
into individual 3/4-cup
capacity ovenproof
dishes, place dishes in a
baking tray. Pour warm
water to come halfway
up the sides of dishes.
Bake 45–55 minutes,
or until just set.
4. Remove from oven,
cool. When cool,
refrigerate until quite
cold. This will take
at least 3 hours.

When ready to serve,
sprinkle each of the
custards with a thin
layer of brown sugar
and place under very
hot preheated grill for
1–2 minutes or until
sugar turns to caramel,
watching them very
carefully. The brown
sugar burns extremely
quickly, similar to
toffee. Use tongs
or oven mitts to
handle dishes. Cool
before serving.

Jewelled Pavlova

Preparation time:
30 minutes
Total cooking time:
2 hours
+ cooling
Serves 8–10

6 egg whites
1 1/2 cups caster sugar
1 teaspoon cornflour
1 teaspoon vanilla
   essence
1 teaspoon white wine
   vinegar

Filling
1 1/4 cups cream,
   whipped
1 teaspoon icing
   sugar
250 g punnet
   strawberries
2 kiwi fruit, peeled and
   sliced
2 passionfruit

1. Preheat oven to
very slow 120°C.
Brush a 32 x 28 cm
oven tray with melted
butter or oil. Line
with baking paper.
Mark a 20 cm circle
on paper. In large dry
mixing bowl, beat egg
whites with electric
beaters until stiff
peaks form. Gradually
add sugar, beating
constantly until
mixture is thick and
glossy and all sugar is
dissolved. Add
cornflour, essence
and vinegar, beat
until combined.
2. Spoon meringue
into piping bag, fitted
with a star-shaped
nozzle. Pipe an outer
ring onto the circle
on prepared tray. Fill
in the ring with piped
meringue. Bake for
1 1/2–2 hours or until
pale and crisp. Turn
off oven and allow
meringue to cool
completely in oven,
with door slightly
ajar. Transfer to a
serving platter.
3. *To make filling:*
Combine cream
and icing sugar. Fill
the centre of the
pavlova with cream.
Remove stalks from
strawberries. Arrange
strawberries, slices of
kiwi fruit and pulp of
passionfruit on top.

Jewelled Pavlova (top) and Crème Brûlée.

Apple and Mixed Fruit Pie

Preparation time:
 50 minutes
Total cooking time:
 35–40 minutes
Serves 10

Pastry
1 cup plain flour
1/2 cup self-raising flour
2 tablespoons caster
 sugar
pinch salt
125 g butter, chopped
1 egg yolk
1–2 tablespoons cold
 water

Filling
1 kg Granny Smith
 apples
1/2 cup sultanas
1/2 cup chopped pecan
 nuts
1/2 cup chopped dates
1/4 cup soft brown
 sugar
1 teaspoon grated
 lemon rind
1 tablespoon orange
 marmalade
1 teaspoon ground
 cinnamon
1/3 cup plain flour
45 g butter, cut into
 cubes
1 tablespoon milk
1 tablespoon sugar

1. Preheat oven to
moderate 180°C. Brush
a 23 cm round pie dish
(4–5 cm deep) with
melted butter or oil.

2. *To make pastry:* In
processor bowl, place
flours, sugar, salt and
butter and process 30
seconds or until
mixture is fine and
crumbly. Add egg yolk
and a little water,
process 20 seconds
or until mixture just
comes together. Turn
onto lightly floured
surface. Knead gently
1–2 minutes or until
mixture forms a ball.
Cover with plastic
wrap, refrigerate for
15 minutes.
3. *To make filling:* Peel
the apples, core and cut
into small pieces. In
large bowl, place
apples, sultanas,
pecans, dates, brown
sugar, rind, marmalade,
cinnamon, flour and
butter. Mix well. Place
apple mixture into
prepared dish. Roll a
quarter of the pastry
between two sheets of
plastic wrap into a long
thin strip. Press strip
around edge of the pie
dish. Roll remaining
pastry large enough to
cover top of pie. Trim
excess pastry and pinch
edges decoratively.
4. Brush top of pie
with milk; sprinkle
with sugar. Cut two or
three slashes in top of
pastry. Bake 35–40
minutes or until skewer
inserted in the centre
shows the apple is
cooked – it should be
firm but not crisp.
Leave to rest 10
minutes before cutting.
Dust with icing sugar.
Serve with cream.

Baked Rice Custard

Preparation time:
 20 minutes
Total cooking time:
 1 hour
Serves 4

1/4 cup shortgrain rice
2 eggs
1/4 cup caster sugar
1 1/2 cups milk
1/2 cup cream
1–2 teaspoons grated
 lemon rind
1 teaspoon vanilla
 essence
1/4 cup sultanas or
 currants (optional)
1/4 teaspoon ground
 nutmeg or cinnamon

1. Preheat oven to
moderately slow
160°C. Brush a deep,
20 cm round
ovenproof dish
(1.5 L capacity) with
melted butter or oil.
2. Cook rice in medium
pan of boiling water
until just tender; drain.
3. In a medium mixing
bowl, whisk the eggs,
sugar, milk, cream, rind
and essence for about
2 minutes. Fold in the
cooked rice and
sultanas or currants.

Baked Rice Custard (top) and Apple and Mixed Fruit Pie.

Pour mixture into the prepared dish. Sprinkle with nutmeg or cinnamon.

4. Place filled dish into deep baking dish. Pour in water to come halfway up the sides. Bake for 50 minutes or until custard is set and a knife comes out clean when inserted in the centre. Remove dish from baking dish immediately. Let stand 5 minutes before serving. Serve with cream or stewed fruits.

Apricot Gateau

Preparation time:
55 minutes +
refrigeration
Total cooking time:
30 minutes
Serves 6–8

1/3 cup plain flour
1/3 cup cornflour
150 g unsalted butter
1/4 cup caster sugar
7 eggs, separated
1/3 cup caster sugar,
   extra
30 g ground
   hazelnuts
orange rind to
   garnish

Filling

500 g dried apricots
1 teaspoon vanilla
   essence
1½ cups water
2 tablespoons grated
   orange rind
1–2 teaspoons curaçao
1 cup cream

1. Preheat oven to moderate 180°C. Line three 20 x 30 cm cake tins with baking paper. Sift flours three times onto a sheet of greaseproof paper.
2. Using electric beaters, beat butter and sugar in a small bowl until light and creamy. Add the egg yolks one at a time, beating well after each addition. Transfer to a large bowl.
3. Beat egg whites until stiff peaks form. Gradually add extra sugar, beat until mixture is thick and glossy and all sugar is dissolved. Using a metal spoon, fold flours, hazelnuts and egg whites into butter mixture.
4. Spread mixture in prepared tins. Bake for 15–20 minutes or until the cakes are golden and spring back when lightly touched. Cool in tins for 5 minutes. Turn onto wire racks.

5. *To make filling:* Place apricots, essence and water in a medium pan. Cook over medium heat for 5–10 minutes until very soft. Remove from heat, cool slightly. Place apricot mixture, rind and curaçao in food processor, process 20 seconds or until smooth. Set aside to cool.
6. *To assemble cake:* Trim outer edges of each cake. Cut each cake into three 10 x 20 cm pieces. Sandwich layers together with apricot filling, ending with cake on top. Reserve a little filling for joining. Wrap in plastic wrap and refrigerate 20 minutes. Remove wrap and place cake on the edge of the bench. Using a serrated edged knife, cut diagonally from the top right-hand corner towards the bottom left-hand corner. Place a ruler on the top right-hand corner to use as a guide. Turn out cakes,

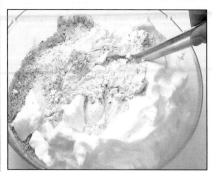

1. *Using a metal spoon, fold flours, hazelnuts and egg whites into butter.*

2. *Process apricot mixture, rind and curaçao for 20 seconds or until smooth.*

Apricot Gateau.

so that stripes run vertically and cake has a pyramid shape. Sandwich together with remaining filling. Beat cream until firm peaks form, spread over cake. Pipe rosettes or swirls along the top centre. To serve, cut into slices and decorate with shreds of orange rind.

3. When cakes are cooled, cut each into three 10 cm x 20 cm rectangular pieces.

4. Cut diagonally from top right-hand corner towards bottom left-hand corner.

49

Traditional Baked Cheesecake

Preparation time:
  25 minutes
Total cooking time:
  1 hour
Serves 8

Crust
200 g plain biscuits,
  finely crushed
1 teaspoon mixed spice
125 g butter, melted

Filling
3 eggs
³/4 cup caster sugar
500 g cream cheese,
  cut into cubes
1 teaspoon vanilla
  essence
¹/4 cup sultanas
2 teaspoons finely
  grated lemon rind

whipped cream,
  nutmeg, berries,
  for serving

1. Preheat oven to moderate 180°C.
2. *To make crust.* Combine biscuits, mixed spice and butter and press into base and sides of greased 20 cm round springform tin. Smooth out with base of a glass to ensure crust is even.
3. *To make filling:* In a large bowl, beat eggs and sugar with electric beaters until thick and pale and caster sugar has dissolved. Gradually beat in cream cheese. Add essence, sultanas and lemon rind, beat until mixture is smooth and light.
4. Pour mixture into prepared tin. Bake 1 hour or until filling is set. Cool in tin. Spread top with cream. Dust with nutmeg, serve with berries.

Tipsy Cake

Preparation time:
  40 minutes
  + refrigeration
Total cooking time:
  10 minutes
Serves 6–8

1 double unfilled
  sponge
¹/4 cup custard powder
¹/4 cup caster sugar
1 1/2 cups milk
1 teaspoon vanilla
  essence
³/4 cup cream,
  whipped
1/2 cup sherry or other
  liquor
1/2 cup raspberry or
  apricot jam
1 cup cream, extra
250 g punnet
  strawberries, hulled
  and halved, optional
20 green grapes, halved
118 g jar mango
  baby gel

1. Cut each cake in half horizontally. Blend custard powder, sugar and milk in medium pan. Cook, stirring, over medium heat 4–5 minutes or until mixture boils and thickens. Remove from heat. Cover surface with plastic wrap, cool. Remove plastic wrap, fold in vanilla and cream.
2. Line a 20 cm round x 12 cm deep container with plastic wrap. Place one layer of sponge into the base of the container. Brush with one-third of the sherry. Spread over one-third each of the jam and the custard. Repeat layering, ending with cake. Cover and refrigerate several hours or overnight.
3. Turn cake onto serving plate, remove plastic wrap. Beat extra cream until firm peaks form. Spread cream over the top and sides of cake. Pipe rosettes around the edge. Place strawberries, if liked, and grapes at random over the top to decorate. Heat baby gel in microwave oven or a small pan over medium heat until melted. Brush lightly over fruits. Cut into wedges to serve.

Traditional Baked Cheesecake (top)
and Tipsy Cake.

Zabaglione

Preparation time:
  20 minutes
Total cooking time:
  15 minutes
Serves 2–4

4 egg yolks
¼ cup sugar
¼ cup Cointreau
¼ cup blood orange
  juice
wafers for serving

1. Using electric beaters, beat egg yolks and sugar until thick and pale.
2. Stand over pan of simmering water and continue beating until mixture is thick and fluffy and increased in volume.
3. Gradually add combined Cointreau and juice in a thin stream. Continue beating for 10 minutes. If mixture begins to cook on sides of bowl, remove from heat for a few seconds, then return. Pour mixture into shallow parfait or champagne glasses. Serve with wafers.

Note: Blood oranges are sweeter, with reddish flesh. If not available, use ordinary oranges.

Lemon Curd Tart with Candied Rind

Preparation time:
  40 minutes
Total cooking time:
  1 hour 15 minutes
Serves 6–8

Sweet shortcrust pastry
120 g butter,
  chopped
1–1½ cups plain flour
2 tablespoons sugar
3 egg yolks
2–3 tablespoons chilled
  water

Filling
¼ cup lemon juice
3 teaspoons grated
  lemon rind
3 eggs
⅔ cup caster sugar
⅔ cup cream

Candied rind
1 cup caster sugar
¼ cup water
rind of 3 lemons
rind of 3 limes

1. Preheat oven to moderately hot 210°C (190°C gas). Brush 23 cm round fluted flan tin with melted butter or oil.
2. *To make pastry:* Using fingertips, rub the butter into the flour for 1–2 minutes or until mixture is fine and crumbly. Stir in sugar, egg yolks and enough water for mixture to form a firm dough. Press mixture together to form a ball. Wrap in plastic wrap and refrigerate 15 minutes. Roll dough, between two sheets of baking paper, large enough to cover base and sides of tin. Trim edges. Cover pastry-lined tin with sheet of greaseproof paper. Spread a layer of dried beans or rice evenly over paper. Bake 20–25 minutes. Remove from oven; discard paper and beans/rice. Bake further 5 minutes or until golden. Cool.
3. *To make filling:* In bowl, whisk together all filling ingredients. Pour mixture into pastry case. Reduce oven to slow 150°C. Bake for 50 minutes or until curd has set in the middle. Allow to cool.
4. *To make candied rind:* Combine sugar and water in heavy-based pan. Stir over low heat without boiling until sugar has dissolved. Add rind, bring to boil, reduce heat and simmer for 10 minutes. Remove from heat, cool. Drain, reserve syrup. Decorate outer edge with rosettes of whipped cream. Arrange candied rind over cream. Serve with reserved syrup if desired.

*Zabaglione (top)
and Lemon Curd Tart with Candied Rind.*

Classic Chocolate Mousse

Preparation time:
  25 minutes
Total cooking time:
  5 minutes +
  2 hours refrigeration
Serves 6

200 g dark chocolate,
  chopped
40 g unsalted butter
1 tablespoon icing sugar
1 teaspoon vanilla
  essence
4 eggs, separated
2/3 cup cream, whipped
1 tablespoon brandy,
  cognac or orange
  liqueur
whipped cream, extra,
  for serving

1. Place chocolate in heatproof bowl. Stand over pan of simmering water and stir until chocolate has melted and is smooth. Remove from heat. Cool slightly.
2. Using electric beaters, beat butter, sugar and essence until light and creamy. Add yolks, one at a time, beating well after each addition. Add chocolate; beat until smooth. Fold in a third of the cream.
3. Place egg whites in small dry mixing bowl. Beat until stiff peaks form. Using a metal spoon, fold egg whites, remaining cream and liqueur into chocolate mixture. Pour mixture into individual glasses. Refrigerate 2 hours or until set. Serve with cream.

French Fruit Flan

Preparation time:
  45 minutes
Total cooking time:
  45 minutes
Serves 8–10

Sweet shortcrust pastry
120 g butter, chopped
1½ cups plain flour
2 tablespoons sugar
3 egg yolks

Custard
2 egg yolks
¼ cup sugar
¼ cup plain flour
1½ cups milk
2 teaspoons vanilla
  essence

Topping
¾ cup apricot jam
fruits such as kiwi fruit,
  strawberries, tinned
  apricots, grapes

1. *To make pastry:* Using fingertips, rub butter into flour until mixture is fine and crumbly. Stir in sugar and egg yolks. Press mixture together to form a ball and refrigerate in plastic wrap for 30 minutes.
2. Roll pastry between two sheets of baking paper, making the pastry large enough to cover base and sides of a greased 23 cm fluted flan tin. Trim edges. Cut sheet of greaseproof paper to cover pastry-lined tin. Spread a layer of dried beans or rice evenly over paper. Bake 20–25 minutes. Remove from oven; discard paper and beans/rice. Bake for a further 5 minutes. Allow to cool.
3. *To make custard:* In medium bowl, whisk egg yolks, sugar and flour until thick and pale. Heat milk in pan until almost boiling; remove from heat. Add milk gradually to egg mixture, beating constantly. Return mixture to pan. Stir constantly over medium heat 5 minutes or until custard boils and thickens. Remove from heat; add essence. Cover with plastic wrap; cool.
4. *To make topping:* Heat jam gently over low heat until it simmers. Strain and brush inside of pastry case with one-quarter of jam. Spread custard over jam. Cut fruit into thin slices, arrange over custard. Brush the fruit with remaining warm jam. Refrigerate.

French Fruit Flan (top) and Classic Chocolate Mousse.

Macerated Berries with Mascarpone

Preparation time:
  20 minutes
Total cooking time:
  10 minutes
Serves 4–6

1 cup blackberries
1 cup raspberries
1 cup blueberries
1 cup loganberries or
  similar berries
1–2 tablespoons caster
  sugar
2 oranges
1/3 cup water
2 tablespoons sugar
mascarpone, lightly
  stirred

1. Combine all berries in a bowl, sprinkle caster sugar over, toss lightly. Cover, refrigerate.
2. Peel oranges and cut rind into long thin strips.
3. Combine water and sugar in small pan, stir over low heat until sugar dissolves. Add prepared orange rind, simmer gently 1–2 minutes or until just tender. Cool.
4. Reserve one tablespoon of the orange strips. Combine remaining orange strips and cooking syrup with the berries, mix lightly.
5. To serve, spoon cherry mixture into goblets. Garnish with mascarpone and reserved orange rind strips.

Blackberry and Two Fruit Trifle

Preparation time:
  40 minutes +
  overnight refrigeration
Total cooking time:
  10 minutes
Serves 4–6

2 x 85 g packets
  blackberry jelly
1 sponge cake
1/3 cup marsala or
  sherry
1/4 cup blackberry jam
425 g can peaches,
  drained, chopped
425 g can pears,
  drained, chopped

Custard
3 egg yolks
1/4 cup sugar
2 tablespoons plain flour
1 1/2 cups milk
1/4 cup cream
1 teaspoon vanilla
  essence
whipped cream, extra,
  for serving
blackberries for
  decoration

1. Make jelly according to instructions on packet. Pour mixture into a 28 x 18 cm rectangular tin. Refrigerate until set. Cut sponge into 1.5 cm cubes. Combine liquor and jam in small pan. Stir over low heat until jam has dissolved. Remove from heat. Place half the sponge cubes in the base of a 12-cup capacity glass bowl. Brush with half the jam mixture. Cover and refrigerate.
2. To make custard: Using electric beaters, beat yolks, sugar and flour 3–5 minutes or until pale and thick. Heat milk in medium pan until almost boiling. Pour milk into yolk mixture, beat well. Return mixture to pan. Stir over low heat 3–4 minutes or until thick. Remove from heat, stir in cream and vanilla, mix well. Cover surface with plastic wrap to prevent a skin forming. Cool.
3. Using a plastic spatula, cut jelly into 1.5 cm cubes. Place cubes on top of sponge alternately with peaches, pears and cold custard. Cover, refrigerate for several hours or overnight. Decorate with cream and blackberries. Dust with icing sugar, if liked.

---

*Macerated Berries with Mascarpone (top)
and Blackberry and Two Fruit Trifle.*

Easy Orange Mousse

Preparation time:
  12 minutes
Total cooking time:
  Nil
Serves 8

1 cup orange juice
2 tablespoons lemon
  juice
2/3 cup caster sugar
1 tablespoon gelatine
1/4 cup water
1 tablespoon orange
  liqueur
3 egg whites
3/4 cup cream,
  whipped until stiff

1. Combine orange and lemon juice in a bowl; add sugar. Leave 10 minutes for the sugar to soften.
2. Sprinkle gelatine over water in a small bowl. Stand in boiling water, stirring until the gelatine has dissolved. Add to juices, with orange liqueur. Mix well. Refrigerate until it is the consistency of unbeaten egg white.
3. Beat orange and lemon jelly mixture until fluffy and light. Using electric beaters, beat egg whites until stiff peaks form. Using a metal spoon, fold the cream and egg whites together. Fold gelatine mixture into egg white mixture.

Spoon into eight individual dessert dishes or wine glasses. The top may be decorated with an orange segment, orange rind and a little whipped cream.

Pears Poached in Red Wine

Preparation time:
  8 minutes + 3–4
  hours refrigeration
Total cooking time:
  20–30 minutes
Serves 4

4 firm pears or 4 firm
  apples
2 cups good claret or
  other red wine
1 cup water
2/3 cup sugar
1 cinnamon stick
2 strips lemon rind
1 tablespoon lemon
  juice
fresh cream for serving

1. Peel pears, leaving the top stalks on. Remove base core with a small melon baller. If using apples, peel and cut into halves; remove the core.
2. Place wine, water, sugar, cinnamon and lemon rind in large pan. Stir over low heat without boiling until sugar is dissolved. Bring slowly to the boil, boil 1 minute. Reduce heat and simmer.

3. Add pears with stalks facing up, or apples. Cover and cook over low heat, pears for 20 minutes and apples for 15 minutes.
4. Using a slotted spoon, remove the fruit carefully to a bowl. Continue simmering the syrup for 6–8 minutes. Add lemon juice, remove from heat; cool slightly. Pour over the fruit. Cover and refrigerate for 3–4 hours before serving. Serve with freshly whipped or clotted cream.

Peach Pastry Pillows

Preparation time:
  45 minutes
Total cooking time:
  30–35 minutes
Serves 8

2 sheets ready rolled
  butter puff pastry
1 egg white, lightly
  beaten
2 teaspoons sugar
2 large peaches
1/3 cup sugar, extra
1 cup water
1/4 cup sweet sherry
4 whole cloves
1/4 teaspoon ground
  cinnamon
1 cup cream, whipped
fruit for serving

1. Preheat oven to moderately hot 210°C (190°C gas). Line a

Clockwise from left: Easy Orange Mousse, Pears Poached in Red Wine and Peach Pastry Pillows.

baking tray with baking paper.
2. Brush one sheet of pastry with egg white. Place other sheet on top. Using 7 cm round fluted, floured cutter, cut eight circles from pastry. Place on tray. Brush with egg white, cut four diagonal slits across top of each round. Sprinkle with sugar. Bake for 10–15 minutes or until golden. Allow to cool.

3. Peel peaches and cut into quarters, remove stones. In pan, combine sugar, water, sherry, cloves and cinnamon. Stir over low heat without boiling until sugar has dissolved. Add peaches. Bring to boil, reduce heat and simmer 5–10 minutes or until peaches are tender. Remove from pan with a slotted spoon. Simmer syrup for further 10–15

minutes or until slightly thickened. Transfer to jug. Cool completely.
4. *To serve:* Split pastry pillows horizontally. Place each base on a serving plate. Slice each peach quarter into four. Lay peach slices over pastry base, fanning out one side. Spoon dollop of cream over. Pour remaining syrup over exposed peaches. Serve with fruit in season.

59

Passionfruit and Citrus Flummery

Preparation time:
35–40 minutes
Total cooking time:
10 minutes +
4 hours chilling
Serves 8

1 tablespoon plain
 flour
1 cup warm water
1 tablespoon gelatine
1/4 cup cold water
1/4 cup lemon juice
2/3 cup orange juice
3/4 cup caster sugar
5 passionfruit

1. In a medium pan,
blend the flour and
warm water to a paste,
adding water a little at a
time. Bring the mixture
to a boil, stirring or
whisking constantly.
Boil for 1 minute,
remove from heat.
2. Sprinkle gelatine
over combined cold
water and lemon juice.
Whisk until gelatine
has dissolved.
3. Add orange juice,
gelatine mixture, sugar
and passionfruit to pan.
Return to heat; bring to
the boil. Transfer
mixture to a large,
heatproof bowl.
4. Stand bowl over ice
cubes, beat with electric
beaters until thick and
light. Transfer mixture
to clean bowl, stand

until beginning to set.
Whisk again lightly to
distribute passionfruit
seeds evenly. Spoon
mixture into individual
parfait glasses. Chill for
about 4 hours or until
lightly set. Serve with
cream if liked.

Walnut Cake with Lemon Syrup

Preparation time:
35 minutes
Total cooking time:
30–40 minutes
Serves 10

1 cup whole walnuts
125 g plain biscuits
1 tablespoon plain flour
1 tablespoon self-
 raising flour
2 teaspoons grated
 lemon rind
3 eggs
1/2 cup sugar

Syrup
1/3 cup water
1/2 cup caster sugar
1/3 cup lemon juice
2 tablespoons dark rum
 or brandy
rind of 1 lemon, finely
 shredded

1. Preheat oven to
moderate 180°C. Brush
a 20 cm round cake tin
with oil. Line base with
baking paper.

2. Place walnuts and
biscuits in food
processor. Process 20
seconds or until finely
crushed. In a bowl,
combine walnut
mixture with flours
and rind.
3. Using electric beaters,
beat eggs and sugar for
5–6 minutes or until
thick and pale.
Gradually fold in nut
mixture. Pour into
prepared tin and
smooth the surface.
Bake 25 minutes or
until skewer comes out
clean when inserted in
centre. Leave cake in
tin. The syrup is poured
over hot cake.
4. *To make syrup:*
Combine water, sugar,
juice and rum or
brandy and rind in
small pan. Stir over low
heat without boiling
until sugar is dissolved.
Bring to boil; reduce
heat, simmer 12–15
minutes. Remove rind
and set aside. Poke
some holes in top of
cake with a fine skewer.
Spoon syrup over cake
and let it soak in.
Continue until all syrup
is absorbed. Leave cake
to cool 10 minutes,
turn onto serving plate.
Cut into wedges and
serve with whipped
cream, if liked, and
candied rind.

---

*Passionfruit and Citrus Flummery (top)
and Walnut Cake with Lemon Syrup.*

Cassata

Preparation time:
  30 minutes +
  24 hours freezing
Total cooking time:
  Nil
Serves 8

750 g rich chocolate
  gelato, softened, or
  chocolate ice-cream
1 stale sponge cake
¼ cup Cointreau
500 g vanilla gelato,
  softened, or vanilla
  ice-cream
2 tablespoons pistachio
  nuts, chopped
2 tablespoons glacé
  cherries, chopped
2 tablespoons mixed
  peel
1 cup mixed berries
3 teaspoons caster sugar

1. Line base and sides of
a 21 x 14 x 7 cm
straight-sided loaf tin
with foil. Place in the
freezer for 3–4 minutes.
2. Spoon three-quarters
of the chocolate gelato
or ice-cream around the
inside edges of chilled
tin, smoothing carefully
until it is even thickness.
Return tin to freezer
until firm.
3. Cut the sponge into
1 cm cubes and toss
lightly in Cointreau.
4. Combine the vanilla
gelato or ice-cream with
the sponge squares,
nuts, cherries and peel.

Spoon mixture into the
loaf tin, smooth off the
top and cover with the
remaining chocolate
gelato or ice-cream.
Return to freezer for at
least 24 hours.
5. Process berries with
caster sugar until
smooth. Serve with
sliced cassata.

Hazelnut Roll with Raspberry Cream

Preparation time:
  30 minutes +
  2 hours refrigeration
Total cooking time:
  37 minutes
Serves 8

¾ cup roasted hazelnuts
5 eggs, separated
¾ cup sugar
1 teaspoon vanilla
  essence
⅓ cup self-raising flour
1 tablespoon plain flour

Raspberry Cream
⅓ cup cream
200 g punnet
  raspberries, lightly
  mashed
1 tablespoon caster
  sugar
1 tablespoon brandy

1. Preheat oven to a
moderate 180°C. Brush
a 30 x 25 x 2 cm Swiss

roll tin with oil. Line
base and sides with
paper; grease paper.
Place hazelnuts in a food
processor. Process for
15 seconds or until
finely crushed.
2. Beat egg yolks and
sugar with electric
beaters until thick and
pale. Add vanilla.
3. Using electric beaters,
beat whites until they
form stiff peaks. Using a
metal spoon, fold whites
and sifted flours into the
yolks, one-third at a
time. Fold in nuts with
last third. Spoon
mixture into prepared
tin; smooth surface.
Bake 15 minutes or until
lightly golden and
springy to touch. Turn
onto a dry tea-towel
covered with
greaseproof paper and
sprinkled with sugar;
stand 1 minute. Using
the tea-towel as a guide,
carefully roll cake up
with paper; leave for
5 minutes or until cool.
Unroll the cake and
discard paper.
**4. *To make raspberry
cream:*** Beat cream until
stiff peaks form. Fold in
raspberries, sugar and
brandy (cream should
have a marbled look).
Spread cream over cake
leaving a 1.5 cm edge.
Gently re-roll, refrigerate
2 hours before serving.

---

*Hazelnut Roll with Raspberry Cream (top)
and Cassata.*

Index